Making Peace With

Your Emotional Disconnection With Your Parents

A guided journal with 40 prompt questions for understanding, accepting, and grieving your emotionally distant relationship with your parents

by Jasmine Cepeda, LCSW

betternowtherapy.org
Independently Published
Brooklyn, New York

Disclaimer

The information provided in this book is designed to provide helpful information on the topics discussed. This book is not meant to be used, nor should it be used to diagnose or treat any mental health condition. For therapy treatment of any, consult your physician or therapist.

The author is not responsible for any specific mental health issues that may require clinical treatment and is not liable for any damages or negative consequences from any action, application, treatment to any person reading this book. Content is not a substitute for therapy or replacement for formal therapy

Independently Published.

ISBN: 978-1-0879-4292-6

Book Design by Jasmine Cepeda
Fonts Used:
Book Title: Marko One
https://fonts.google.com/specimen/Marko+One
Book Title and Chapter Titles: Bellefair
https://fonts.google.com/specimen/Bellefair
Book Contents: Open Sans
https://fonts.google.com/specimen/Open+Sans

Visit us on the web!
www.betternowtherapy.org

Tag Us!
@betternowtherapy

Dedicated to

the children and
adult children that
feel alone in their
experience.

You are not alone.

Table of Contents

Introduction

As a psychotherapist, I have observed that many folks have trouble making peace with their emotionally disconnected (neglectful or superficial) relationships with their parent/s. They have difficulty tolerating the loss and loneliness that so often describes not having a deep connection.

It can be difficult to understand and accept your emotional detachment from your parents. The unprocessed tension can create obstacles in feeling safe in other relationships, and in reparenting yourself (being there for yourself).

It can be even more difficult to explore your emotional disconnection when it requires coming face to face with the realities of your childhood. Integrating the past into your present experience can be painful.

When folks express lacking emotional depth with their parent/s, they have their specific meaning and memories in mind. Hence, this guide helps you explore your unique meaning and memories.

This guide also focuses on making peace with your reality through building **self-understanding**, **acceptance**, and **mourning**.

One thing this journal does **not** focus on is your parents--why are they the way that they are, and why they did what they did. Many folks who feel emotionally disconnected from their parents already focus **too much** on their parents: *Why are they so distant? Why are they* *so judgemental? Why are they so mean? Why are they so self-centered? Why? Why? Why? And how can I be a better child? How can I help? How can I be there for them? How do they feel? How? How? How? And what do they think of me? What are their needs? What do they want from me? What? What? What?* Hence, this guide is about **you**: ***What do you need? How do you feel?***

This is not to say that your parents do not deserve empathy and understanding (because they do), but it will not be the center of attention in this guide. The first and only question around empathizing with your parents will be towards the end, in the chapter about empathy. **Empathy** is not an excuse but is necessary to accept **ambivalence**, the state of having mixed feelings about something. Nothing is black or white. Most things lie in the gray area. Having unpleasant emotions (like anger, sadness, resentment) does not mean that you cannot also feel pleasant emotions (like empathy, care, and love) towards your parent/s.

This is a guided *journal*. **Journaling** is useful because it is a space for you to work out the things in your head--to express your inner thoughts and feelings. Journaling is a start in increasing your self-understanding and self-validation.

Take your time throughout this guide. There is no need to go through the prompts in any rush. Healing can not be hurried.

Terms in this Guide

"Childhood" in this guide includes the infancy and toddler years. It is used to describe the early period of your life. But when "child" is used, it is not solely meant to identify the time when you were a little kid. That is, "child," in this guide indicates you as your parent's child (adult child).

I use the word "parent/s" to signify your primary childhood caregiver/s (which may have been your parent/s, grandparent/s, adopted parent/s, etc.). And I use both the singular and plural version of parent interchangeably for folks who were raised with a single-parent or only feel emotionally disconnected with one parent. If you feel emotionally disconnected from both of your parents, please remember to journal about **each parent**, not just one.

This guide has 40 questions. Words in **bold** are meant to aid in your journaling exercise. Each journaling question starts off with a general idea, so you can freely write what comes to mind. However, there are follow-up questions that may help. Every question also asks you to *identify your emotions* (or feelings) about what you have written. Additionally, many questions ask about an *associated memory* with your journal entry. Memories can be doors into your emotions.

For brevity, this guide only focuses on emotional neglect and trauma, but other forms of neglect and trauma exist (including neglect of basic needs [like food, shelter, hygiene, etc], and physical, sexual, and financial abuse).

Lastly, thoughts in this guide are based on my personal and professional experience. I reference theories and terms respectively.

What is peace?

Peace is what many of us want in our lives and for the world. Peace comes with a sense of calm, contentment, and equanimity. Peace means the end of fighting and tension.

To be in search of peace in your relationship with your parents means you are **not at peace** with the connection. Having a distressing connection with your parent can be very lonely and painful, but peace is possible. To go towards peace, you must have **hope** that peace is attainable. You must also have the willingness to do the work (or emotional labor) and be resilient.

Journal

1. **What does peace mean to you? What does peace with your relationship with your parents mean to you? What does it look like? How would you feel?**

Journal

Any journey towards peace needs support. If you do not have support, the path towards freedom may feel overwhelming and lonely. Spirituality, friends, therapy, art, music, yoga, exercise, etc. are all forms of helpful support.

In particular, therapy is a valuable kind of support. Feeling emotionally detached, neglected, or estranged from your parent/s can lead to major emotional and psychological distress in other areas in your life. Therapy is a place to take care of your emotional wellbeing and mental health. Therapy is also extremely useful when you have gone through traumatic physical, sexual, or emotional experiences.

Journal

2. **Who or what will make up your support system through your journey towards peace? How do you feel about your support system?**

Your Emotional Disconnection

You've bought this guide because you feel you have an emotional disconnection with your parent/s and you want to find release from the tension of such a relationship! But first, you need to *describe* the pain that is imprisoning you. Below are some words folks use to describe their relationships. Feel free to find your own words too. Words are a powerful tool for self-expression, meaning-making, and self-validation.

- abusive
- aggressive
- annoying
- anxiety-provoking
- careless
- co-dependent
- cold
- confusing
- controlling
- cruel
- closed off
- dissatisfying
- dangerous
- demanding
- dismissive
- distant
- disengaged
- disappointing
- draining
- estranged
- fake
- frustrating
- guarded
- hopeless
- immature
- insensitive
- insecure
- judgemental
- lacking
- lonely
- inconsistent
- inconsiderate
- irresponsible
- manipulative
- mean
- not enough
- narcissistic
- neglectful
- overwhelming
- one-sided
- pseudo
- rejecting
- rigid
- sad
- scary
- self-centered
- shallow
- stressful
- superficial
- tense
- traumatizing
- unsafe
- uneasy
- unpredictable
- untrustworthy
- withholding
- unresponsive

+ words

- affectionate
- caring
- consistent
- easy
- engaged
- enough
- flexible
- fun
- hopeful
- kind
- loving
- non-judgmental
- open
- predictable
- safe
- secure
- supportive
- understanding

Journal

3. **How do you describe your emotionally distant parent/s? Or the relationship? Why? How do you feel about this? How does the relationship feel?**

Journal

Hunger

For A Deep Connection

We are all born with a hunger for human connection. It is human nature to want to connect with others, to move away from loneliness and isolation. It is also natural to want to communicate our emotions to others, and to feel a compassionate, caring response back. Interpersonal needs are crucial for individuals to find meaning and purpose in their lives.

Journal

4. **What (if any) are some memories of feeling emotionally *connected* with your parent/s (in childhood or as an adult)? Why do you think you remember these memories? How do you feel about this?**

The desire for a **deep** (rather than a **shallow**) emotional connection is also normal. The need to be *deeply seen* and *known* by another is a motivation for why many seek deep or **intimate** relationships.

Journal

5. **Do you have** deep **emotional connections with others in your life? Like friends, siblings, partner, or your other parent? If not, how do you feel about his? How can you create** deeper **connections with others?**

It is understandable why anyone would be **restless** and hungry for more if they only have shallow relationships in their life. However, to feel disconnected from the people who brought you into this world can feel even more **tragic**.

A Hollow Connection

All hunger (including the hunger for connection) will find its way to be satisfied (even through unhealthy means). For instance, sometimes hunger becomes its own form of satisfaction, which happens with **depression** (and **eating disorders**). Being filled with **dissatisfaction** and starvation can become a fullness in itself, an **empty** and **hollow** fullness that folks grow accustomed to. It's **numbness**. "Fixing" your hunger with **endless craving** is a form of **self-harm**, **low self-worth**, and **hopelessness** (i.e., depression).

Another example can be seen with folks struggling with **substance abuse**. Their goal is to feel full through getting high. But it's temporary and the cravings are never satisfied--it becomes a permanent chase.

Ultimately, satiating one's hunger with a short-term fix is a form of **distraction, denial,** and **dissociation.**

Hunger is another word for **need**. Hence, not all cessations of hunger or a need are "unhealthy." For example, some pangs of hunger (like for adventure, play, creativity, newness, etc.) are momentary by definition, thus, can be satisfied easily. These fits of hunger also come back in different ways, thus, can be satiated in different ways, unlike some other needs that are defined by their long-term, consistent nature--like love, connection, meaning, purpose, motivation, support, etc.

The next page has a **list** of needs/hungers.

HUNGERS/NEEDS

- adventure
- affection
- alleviation
- appreciation
- attention
- autonomy
- authenticity
- awareness
- bonding experiences
- care
- clarity
- closeness
- comfort
- communication
- compassion
- connection
- consistency
- consideration
- control
- creativity
- distance
- ease
- empathy
- equality
- fun
- help
- hope
- honesty
- independence
- interest
- integrity
- intimacy
- joy
- love
- meaning
- mutuality
- openness
- peace
- pleasure
- power
- pride
- protection
- purpose
- quiet
- relatedness
- reciprocity
- respect
- safety
- sexual needs
- stability
- support
- tenderness
- time to mourn
- to be seen
- to be heard
- to be understood
- to be known
- understanding
- warmth

Basic Needs

- air
- physical safety
- shelter
- sleep
- touch
- water & food

Journal

6. **What other things do you hunger for in your life? (What are your unmet needs, besides emotional intimacy with your parents)?**

How have you "fixed" these hungers or needs? Have you “fixed” your hunger through starvation (being depressed or hopeless)? Explain. How do you feel about this? Have you “fixed” your hunger through temporary solutions (drugs, sex, work, entertainment, busyness?) Explain. How do you feel about this?

Journal

Journal

7. **How has having an emotionally detached relationship with your parent/s affected your hungers/needs? Do you find you need more because of what is missing in your relationship with your parent/s?**

Your Emotional Connection With Yourself

What are emotions?

Simply put, emotions (or feelings) are states of being that are connected to your body and thoughts. Sensations in your body (or thoughts in your mind) can often alert you to how you are feeling.

Emotions are not "good" or "bad," they just are. You do not have to judge yourself for your feelings. Some feelings feel pleasant, while others feel unpleasant. Feelings will give you information about how you are truly experiencing something or someone.

There are thousands of words for feelings. It can be useful to know some of these words to help you verbalize what you are **specifically** experiencing. The next page has a list of emotions, which you can use to help you identify your feelings. Feel free to add more feelings to the list. It is also helpful to know "feeling words," because sometimes your initial feeling about something can be a *concept* or *judgment* (like "shitty" or "bad"), not necessarily a feeling.

Exercise:

One More Time With Feeling
Using the list, look back at your last journal entries and add more feelings!

Feelings

Accepting
Affectionate
Aloof
Ambivalent
Ambitious
Angry
Annoyed
Animosity
Appreciative
Anxious

Ashamed
Betrayed
Brave
Bitter
Calm
Centered
Confident
Connected
Content
Courageous
Cautious

Curious
Delighted
Defeated
Defensive
Distracted
Disappointed
Disconnected
Discouraged
Dissatisfied
Disturbed
Doubtful

Embarrassed
Empathetic
Engaged
Frustrated
Forgiving
Grounded
Guilty
Heartbroken
Hesitant
Helpless

Hopeful
Hopeless
Hostile
Ignored
Indifferent
Impulsive
Insecure
Impatient
Isolated
Jealous
Joyful

Kind
Loving
Moved
Motivated
Nurturing
Open
Optimistic
Overwhelmed
Paralyzed
Provoked
Perplexed

Powerful
Powerless
Regret
Relaxed
Remorse
Restless
Resentful
Sad
Self-conscious
Selfish

Stuck
Shocked
Thankful
Tender
Tired
Touched
Uncentered
Uncomfortable
Uneasy
Ungrounded
Unfulfilled

Unsafe
Unsettled
Understanding
Unstable
Unsure
Vexed
Weary
Withdrawn
Whimsical
Worried
Yearning

Processing & Making Meaning

Processing your feelings is not “doing nothing." Processing your feelings means releasing the **tension**, and finding **alleviation** from what you have been carrying in your mind, body, and soul. The tension that often comes with unpleasant feelings may or may not cease, but it can **lessen** tremendously. What can be transformative about processing your emotions is doing it with someone else (who is empathetic). Those are moments of deep emotional connections. Therapy can be a compassionate space to process your emotions.

Processing your feelings also leads to **making meaning** from your experience, which is crucial for building **self-awareness** and **hope** for the future.

Moreover, processing your emotions is a way to emotionally **connect with yourself**.

Again, you can process your emotions through mindful meditation, but you can also journal or talk with a friend, trusted-person, or therapist. Being vulnerable, and having your emotions understood and validated by someone is an emotionally connecting experience--an experience you do not usually have with your parent/s.

Emotional Regulation

In general, some folks (including your parents) often avoid their feelings because they never learned how to bear their discomfort.

Creating **s p a c e** between feeling and movement is one way to build your tolerance. It especially important to go **s l o w** with your emotions, so you do not get overwhelmed or hurt yourself (or anyone else).

Tolerate yourself and your feelings. Do what your parents could not do for you as a child (**reparent** yourself). Take your emotions seriously.

Having patience, self-compassion, and a non-judgmental attitude towards your feelings helps you to allow and sit with your emotions. This guide invites you to be courageous and get to know yourself through experiencing and staying close to your emotions.

I encourage mindfulness and meditation to help you regulate your emotions and soothe yourself. Jon Kabat Zinn, Pema Chodron, and Thich Nhat Hanh are some authors who have written extensively on how to be present and kind to yourself in any state, including feeling states.

It can be difficult to have emotional regulation skills if your parents did not model healthy forms.

Journal

8. **What ways have you seen your parents regulate their emotions? (examples: screaming, throwing things, hitting, verbally attacking, taking a walk, breathing, etc.)**

Journal

Journal

9. **Do you have memories of your parents soothing you from unpleasant emotions as a child (or as an adult)? How do you feel about these memories?**

Journal

10. **If your parents did *not* soothe you, how would you soothe your emotions as a child (or now, as an adult)? Do you have associated memories of this? How do you feel about this?**

Self-Validation & Reparenting

Validating yourself is crucial in confronting your emotional disconnection with your parents, especially if they did not (and do not) validate your feelings or thoughts. It is important to validate your lived experience, which includes your childhood. Rather than *denying*, *dismissing*, *avoiding*, or *gaslighting* yourself, the questions in this guide asks you to **stop acting like your parents**. The questions ask you to become someone other than whom your parents molded you to be--to be attentive, reliable, patient, and compassionate towards yourself, rather than inattentive, inconsistent, inpatient, and mean to yourself [to **reparent** yourself]. Self-validation and reparenting are encouraged throughout this guide. Part of reparenting means meeting your past unmet childhood needs.

Journal

11. **How do you feel about validating and reparenting yourself?**

Looking at the list of hungers/needs, what are some that you wish to prioritize and meet through your own ways?

Journal

To Be Moved

Feelings and emotions are **moving**-- they are meant to move us and **motivate** our behaviors, thoughts, or perspectives.

When you cut yourself from your feelings, you also cut yourself from the opportunity to be **moved**, to be **touched**, to be **shaken**, to be **changed** by your emotions. If you did not see your parents be moved by your emotions as a child, it can be extremely sad and traumatizing. It can also lead you to model the same behavior towards yourself (**minimizing, neglecting**, or **dismissing** your own emotions).

Internalized Messages

If you have not seen your parent be *moved* by your emotions, you may **internalize** the message that your emotions are **unworthy, unimportant, too much, too uncontrollable, or too intolerable**.

If your parents made it **unsafe** for you to share your feelings, you may also internalize the idea that your feelings are unsafe, causing you to **fear** (or have **anxiety**) about your own emotions.

Lastly, if your parents maintain that being **vulnerable** and **open** with your emotions is a sign of **weakness**, you may internalize that idea as well.

Melanie Klien described internalization (or in her words, **introjection**) as something we all do (unconsciously or not), to make others' behaviors or responses more predictable, less dangerous (1975).

Hence, some children internalize their parents' messages, to make their parents' actions or attitudes more **foreseeable**, less unstable (physically or emotionally). For instance, if a child notices that their parent walks away every time he cries, he may internalize the message: "My dad can't handle my crying. I'm disappointed. In the future, I can't go to him. And if he can't handle my sadness, others can't too." Thus, the child **avoids** feeling emotionally unsafe and unstable, by *predicting (or internalizing)* that others won't be able to handle his sadness.

Another example: a teenager who realizes that every time she expresses her anger, her mother hits her, may internalize the message, "I can't be angry (or express my anger) with my mother, or anyone because it is dangerous. My anger hurts me. My anger is not valid."

Below are more examples of common internalized messages from emotionally disconnected parents:

I'm:	My feelings:
aloof	cause problems
annoying	don't matter
asking for too much	take too much time
boring	are: inconvenient
cold	invalid
distracted	not serious
inconsiderate	not enough
not interesting	shameful
too sensitive	unimportant
unsympathetic	uncontrollable
unloveable	unbearable
undeserving	wrong

Reference:
Melanie Klein, *The Psychoanalysis of Children*, trans. Alix Strachey (London: The Hogarth Press, 1975)

Journal

12. **What are some messages about your emotions (or about yourself) that you have internalized from your parents? What are your associated memories from childhood (or present)? How do you feel about this?**

Journal

As one can see, internalized messages influence one's future behaviors, feelings, and personalities (positively and negatively). Therapy can help you explore the long-term effects of your internalizations.

Journal

13. **How have internalized messages from your parents, influenced your personality, behavior, and feelings? How do you feel about this?**

Journal

Sharing Your True Self

Emotions are expressions of our identity and self. When your parent does not acknowledge your emotion, they are not acknowledging you! You do not feel seen or heard.

When they do not show genuine interest, concern, or empathy, but show judgement, criticism, or distance you do not feel safe to express your true emotions, and this becomes an obstacle for expressing **your true self**.

All of this can feel dissatisfying, lonely, and sad. It becomes hard to share both your joys and disappointments because in either case, your parent does not make you feel safe. You do not show your parent the authentic, full version of you because of their unpleasant reactions when you try. They get the edited version of you, while you hold your tongue about how you really feel or what's really going on in your life.

In the end, what you're stuck with is connecting with your parent/s around emotions that you have learned *they're* comfortable with, that *they* can tolerate. These moments with them may not be as satisfying because they're **shallow,** and not around emotions you are really feeling! **You cannot be real**! It's **fake**, **inauthentic**, and **ingenuine**.

Being authentic to yourself is a way to emotionally **connect with yourself**! Finding **others** that you can be genuine with is also important and transformative!

Journal

14. **Who are you truly? What are some emotions, interests, or personality traits that you do not show to your parent/s? How do you feel about this?**

Journal

15. **How do you feel about not being able to be your *full, true* self around your parent/s? What is it about your parent's behavior (or lack thereof) that makes you not share your true self? Do they not ask, are they judgemental, mean, etc.)**

What parts of your true self *can* you show your parent/s (if any) Why? How do you feel about this?

Journal

A Shallow Connection

A **disconnection** is a *connection* defined by what is **absent,** hence, it is still a connection. For example, some disconnections are actually connections **tethered** by traumatic experiences (through the *absence* of safety and hope).

Meanwhile, a connection is a connection defined by what is **present**, what is there.

Though you may be aware of what is lacking in your relationship with your parent/s, you may be blind to what is *present* (even if it's superficial elements).

Journal

16. **What is** *present* **in your relationship with your parent/s? How do you feel about this? Is there more that is present than** *absent***? How do you feel about this? Would you describe your relationship with your parents as** shallow**? Explain.**

Journal

Some folks are content with a **shallow** connection with their parents (especially if they've found deep connections elsewhere in their life).

Accepting a superficial relationship can only occur when one accepts **ambivalence** (which will be explored later in the guide). Accepting ambivalence means accepting the **dissatisfaction** and **hunger** for more, while also **acknowledging** and **appreciating** what does exist. Moments of connection *can* happen with your parents, though they may not be as deep as you want. The hunger for more may always bring you **sadness** and dissatisfaction, but it does not need to take away from the small, but pleasant feelings experienced in their presence (if any exist).

Everyone has different definitions of what a "superficial" relationship with their parents looks like. For some, taking a quiet walk with their parent is not a surface-level connection, while for others it is.

Journal

17. **Looking at the list of needs, what needs of *yours* (if any) are being filled by having a superficial relationship with your patent/s?**

18. **Looking at the list of needs, what needs of your *parents* (if any) are being filled by having a superficial relationship with them?**

Journal

19. **By having said superficial relationship, are you taking more care of your parent's needs or your own? How do you feel about this?**

A Disconnection

Expressing your emotions is an attempt to connect, to be seen, heard, and understood by another. If you ever felt **ignored**, **dismissed**, or **misunderstood** by someone while sharing your feelings, it was a **disconnection**. They did not *connect* to your emotions. You were left feeling **unseen, disappointed, detached,** and maybe even **withdrawn** and **sad.**

As you can see, **an emotional disconnection** is a **failed opportunity** to soothe, acknowledge, and empathize with someone's emotions. It is a **rupture. fracture, and disturbance in the existing connection**. When you have many of these failed moments with someone, it creates a *general sense* of being emotionally disconnected from that person.

Emotionally **invalidating** experiences with your parents deepen (or start) the rupture in the bond. The fracture can only be repaired (or made worse) by your parent's future emotional responses. The disturbance (regardless if your bond is shallow or deep) needs to be mended. And if it is not, your feelings of **discomfort** and **insecurity** around your parents will **define** the relationship. Your relationship (even if it's a superficial one) will begin to **diminish** even further.

Again, the disconnection in the relationship is on your parents to restore, that is, if they're the ones hurting you. As an imperfect being, you may also hurt your parents (and others)--in these cases, you too need to do the work to repair the disconnection.

Journal

20. **Can you remember a time when you expressed a feeling to your parents, and they did** *not* **express adequate empathy, validation, and acknowledgment for your emotions? Write about this memory. (This was you trying to connect and they dropped the ball).**

Journal

21. **What is a memory of your parents emotionally** *repairing* **a disconnection? Or a memory of them acknowledging your feelings and being compassionate and soothing? How do you feel about this? If you don't have such memories, how do you feel about this?**

Childhood Emotional Regulation

The only exception when it is understandable and normal to be insensitive (or even mean) towards your parents (and others) is during your childhood, pre-teen, and teenage years (basically, while you're in your parent's care). Childhood, especially, is the time where you **learn** about your emotions and how to soothe yourself. But kids can only learn how to **soothe** themselves (in healthy ways) through **expressing** their emotions. While feeling their feelings, kids may say mean things, have tantrums, or cry excessively--because they're *learning*--they're experiencing emotions for the **very first time** and learning how to soothe themselves (Winnicott, 1953; Bowlby, 1959).

Parents need to let their kids be (temporarily) insensitive, mean, and angry (and ideally, mainly to them) so they can experience expressing and tolerating their emotions with a **safe** person, and learn how to **soothe** their feelings. Parents need to put *their* feeling to the side and **help** their children cope with their emotions (Winnicott, 1953; Bowlby, 1959)

However, if parents **guilt-trip** or **excessively shame** their child for not knowing how to handle their feelings, the child may grow up with a **complex** (or tension) about emotions--that they're **too scary, too much, or too uncontrollable**. Because their parents could not tolerate it, they believe their feelings are intolerable. This connects back to how messages are internalized by children.

These children may also grow up **too worried** about hurting others' feelings, which makes them put the feelings of others above their own (*building a martyr complex, or being prone to being taken advantage of, easily guilt-tripped, or pushed-over*). This phenomenon may be exactly what these parents **want** and need because *they* were never taught how to handle *their* emotions (let alone, their child's) (Winnicott, 1953; Bowlby, 1959).

Ideally, parents (and society) would acknowledge and tolerate a child's emotions, while not taking it personally when they act out (i.e., say "I hate you" or punch a wall). The job of parents (and society) is to teach children emotional regulation skills through modeling, discipline, and consequences. But what I'm describing is a perfect world, parents (and society) are not perfect.

Journal

22. Crying is one major way kids express and soothe themselves. If your parents did not make it safe for you to express your emotions (or cry), you may have soothed yourself in unhealthy ways (biting your nails, sucking your thumb, hitting, throwing things, repressing your emotions etc.). **How did you soothe yourself as a child? Do you have associated memories with this?**

Journal

Understanding Your Childhood Attachment

Infants and children need to feel secure in their caregiver's ability to meet both their basic (food, shelter, safety, etc.) and emotional needs (comfort, care, attention, etc) (Bowlby, 1969). For example, a baby may feel discomfort (maybe he has wet his pamper or is scared). He may signal this in many ways. One way is by crying. Parents need to respond to this signal and need to *feel the need to respond*. Sadly, not all parents feel the need (Bowlby, 1969). Some parents may be preoccupied with their own emotions, problems, or childhood traumas. Or, some parents may have a mental health disorder (like depression, bipolar, or substance abuse).

Infants and children are small, helpless, vulnerable, dependent beings that require a lot of care, focus, and attention. Infants especially, cannot do anything for themselves. Parents need to act when their infant or child signals that they are suffering (Winnicott, 1953).

With that said, while being constantly attended to, children may start to grow unrealistic fantasies about their parents (which is normal). They may begin to idealize their parents and look up to them as people who are "always there for me," and never disappointing. For example, a three-year-old may think: "My mom is so great! She always has food for me, plays with me, and buys me my favorite toys! And she always kisses my boo-boos."

However, a gradual **de-romanticization** is also normal and *necessary*--but parents need to create a safe foundation for kids to do that! This is where Donald Winnocott's famous "good-enough" parent comes in. Winnicott was a British pediatrician, psychoanalysis, and researcher who coined the term "good-enough mother" in 1953. He studied families and realized that children need their parents to be **reliable** and **consistent** *most of the time*, in order for the child to eventually feel safe with their **imperfect parent**, **imperfect selves**, and **imperfect word** (Winnicott, 1953).

It's normal for parents to make mistakes and get frustrated. No one is perfect. Raising a child is not easy and requires a lot of work. It is unrealistic for parents to be "on" 24/7, but they need to be "on" *enough of the time*, so their child feels enough **trust** that their needs will be met.

With this feeling of **reliability**, a **secure attachment** grows. Children feel safe to slowly de-romanticize their parents, and slowly accept that the world doesn't revolve around them--every request they want cannot be met (especially not right away), but it does not mean that mommy is "horrible" or that the world is unkind or scary (Winnicott, 1953; Bowlby, 1969). The child slowly realizes that their parent is also a human being and not just their "mommy" or "daddy"--they have other roles, and other relationships (like with their other parent, or other sibling/s). The child learns to tolerate disappointments in their parents, in turn, disappointment in themselves, and in life. The child does not feel valid **hopelessness**, **dread,** or **rage,** since their parent is there enough of the time (Winnicott, 1955-6; Bowlby, 1969).

In order for children to accept that their parents are not the idealized superheroes they wished, children also need to be allowed to express their frustrations and disappointments to their parents, and their parents need to **tolerate, attune,** and be **empathetic.** Even if the child is angry about something relatively inconsequential or small, it may not feel insignificant for the child. The parent needs to be able to **regulate their own emotions**, to be there for their child, and model soothing strategies (Winnicott, 1953; Bowlby, 1959). For example, a four-year-old who gets very angry with their parent for ruining his favorite teddy bear in the washing machine needs compassion and understanding, not anger or insensitivity. Even if the parent is feeling very annoyed with their child's tantrum, the parent needs to pause their own feelings (most of the time) and be empathetic and soothing towards their child.

Securely attached kids know that expressing their unpleasant feelings will not threaten their parents (making them neglectful, aggressive, or rejecting). They also know that showing their emotions will not be a threat to their basic or emotional needs (Bowlby, 1959). In the end, these children trust that their imperfect parents are **predictable**, **reliable**, and **responsive enough**.

A secure childhood attachment with one's parents usually leads to a secure attachment in adulthood. Securely attached adults accept the imperfections and flaws in their parents, themselves, and in the world, especially because they feel there are **enough** positives that outweigh the negatives (helping them to also accept **ambivalence [having mixed feelings]**).

What's more, having a secure attachment with "good enough" parents creates adults with realistic self-esteem (not too self-attacking, not too grandiose). These children also build healthy, authentic selves, with genuine interests and friends. They are free to be who they truly are because their parents welcome and accept them for who they truly are. They feel secure. They feel they are enough. They do not need to over-achieve or over-compensate. They feel they are worthy. They do not self-criticize (Winnicott, D.W., 1955-6).

Journal

23. **Do you feel you had a secure attachment in childhood? If not, what memories remind you that you did not.**

References:
Bowlby, J. (1959). Separation anxiety. International Journal of Psycho-Analysts, XLI, 1-25.
Winnicott, D.W. (1955-6) Clinical varieties of transference. International Journal of Psycho-Analysis, 37, 386
Winnicott, D. (1953). Transitional objects and transitional phenomena, International Journal of Psychoanalysis, 34:89-97

Insecure Attachments in Childhood

As previously noted, it is normal for children to idealize their parents and see them as superheroes (for a period of time). However, when the fantasy ends too early or abruptly, it can be overwhelming, scary, and traumatizing (causing an insecure and unstable attachment). If a baby or child does not feel secure or safe with their caregiver, they will form insecure attachments (Ainsworth et al, 1978; Bowlby, 1969).

Because their parents are not "good-enough," and are dismissive, rejecting, aggressive, or invalidating, a child may feel restrained in (or scared to) express disappointment and fondness towards their parents. In insecure attachments, the parent is **not good enough** in creating a consistent, safe, and tender foundation for their child. Though the parent may meet their child's basic needs (food, shelter, hygiene, etc.), they may fall short meeting their emotional needs.

For instance, if an infant senses their caregiver's physical absence, emotional neglect, or anger, the infant will get upset (whether they show it externally by crying or keep it internally). They are upset because they do not feel safe. They are scared. "Who is going to feed me? If no one loves me, who is going to clean me? I need to be loved for my survival!" If they do not sense that their caregiver is there for both their basic and emotional needs, they do not feel they can trust their caregiver. Thus, the child's only option for survival is to find some other way to feel secure, to relate to their caregiver (be it as unhealthy as it may be). The child is in survival mode (Ainsworth et al, 1978; Bowlby, 1969).

Researchers have described such attachments towards caregivers as: **ambivalent** (or anxious), **avoidant**, or **disorganized** (Ainsworth et al, 1978; Bowlby, 1969).

An infant or child with an **ambivalent** (or **anxious**) **attachment** may have mixed feelings about their caregiver and behave inconsistently because of their caregiver's inconsistencies (sometimes attentive and warm, sometimes neglectful and cold). The child can appear nervous, clingy, and have trouble focusing. The child may behave clingy because they latch on when the parent is in a "good mood," not knowing for how long it will last, or when it will "switch" (Ainsworth et al, 1978).

When the caregiver appears cold or the warmth is nowhere to be found, the child may fear that their caregiver has "stopped loving me," which may then cause the child to "try to get their love back," in unhealthy ways (like pleasing their parent, being a "good little girl" or "good little boy," or even yelling or having a tantrum to get their care and attention etc.) (Ainsworth et al, 1978).

A child with an **avoidant** attachment may not show much emotion towards their caregiver and may avoid affection or closeness. They do this, not because they do not have emotions or do not want closeness, but because their caregiver is emotionally cold, hostile, dismissive, or rejecting. Thus, the child responds with the same emotional detachment, and sometimes anger. "I don't need you!" These kids start to believe that others cannot be relied on, or others can not handle their emotions. They can become highly independent or self-reliant emotionally, especially since the parent has forced them to be. But they can also avoid an emotional connection with themselves (repressing or denying their emotions) (Ainsworth et al, 1978).

A child with a **disorganized** attachment may have paradoxical ways of behaving and relate to their caregiver based on fear. The child is confused and apprehensive about going to their caregiver for comfort because the caregiver is unpredictable; going from caring (safe) to often terrifying and dangerous (not safe). These children grow up in very abusive childhoods, where their caregiver is aggressive and harsh, but, out of nowhere, can be kind. The child can appear frozen (emotionally and physically), and highly anxious when someone tries to care for them (because care becomes associated with abuse). These children may become passive, cold, angry, or depressed. They may seek closeness, but to an extent, because they do not trust it (Ainsworth et al, 1978).

A baby or child who grows up with any of the insecure attachments just described may form coping strategies to relieve their anxiety (such as crying, having outbursts, being distant, having obsessive behaviors [like biting nails, skin-picking, pulling hair, etc.) These coping styles, be them "difficult" for the caregiver as they may be, are attempts to get at least some of their needs met (like attention, comfort, or space).

References:
Ainsworth, M. D. S., Blehar, M. C., Waters, E., & Wall, S. (1978). Patterns of attachment: A psychological study of the strange situation. Oxford, England: Lawrence Erlbaum.
Bowlby, J. (1969). Attachment and loss: Vol. I. Attachment. New York: Basic Books.

Sadly, parents who are not attuned to their child's needs may be blocked by their own childhood traumas to tune in.

Whatever the reason for their emotional neglect or emotional distance (be it past traumas, substance abuse, or a mental health disorder), it was not your fault and you did not deserve it!

Lastly, an insecure childhood attachment affects a child pre-teen and teenage years, influencing their behavior in school, friendships, romantic relationships, and their general feelings and beliefs about the world.

Therapy can help in identifying and exploring your childhood attachment.

Journal

24. **What attachment style do you think you had as a child? Why? How do you feel about this? Do you have any associated memories?**

Journal

Journal

25. **How do you think your childhood attachment style has affected your life (friendships, romantic relations, views of the world, etc.) How do you feel about this? Do you have any associated memories?**

Unmet Childhood Needs

Journal

26. **Looking at the list of needs, what were some of your unmet childhood needs? How do you feel about this?**

Journal

27. **How can you try to meet these needs now (as an adult) and reparent your** inner child**?**

Your Disconnected Family

Parents create and shape their (nuclear) **family's way of being**. As the pioneering family researcher, Salvador Minuchin, conceptualized, families are **systems**--they create their own norms, rules, and boundaries, and **seek stability** (be it through unhealthy means or not) (Minuchin, 1974). Researchers call this ***homeostasis*** (Jackson, 1957). Family's **resist change** to maintain the balance or *homeostasis* in the family.

Therefore, if your parents have created a foundation of distance, superficiality, and dishonesty, your attempt to be close, deep, and honest can entirely threaten and shaken the family base. You can cause distress and fragility within the whole. In other words, in a *disconnected* family, any efforts to be *connected* may intimidate the family structure. Ultimately, a distant family system wants to stay distant for a sense of **equilibrium** and *homeostasis* **(Jackson, 1957).** Although change is necessary for growth, dysfunctional families lack flexibility (Minuchin, 1974).

Family therapy may help in increasing flexibility and finding new ways of relating, that is, if all members want to attend therapy and do the work to change.

Without professional intervention, you can become the **lonely outcast** with your parents and in your family (since your desires are the only ones that no longer fit with the family's *homeostasis (*Jackson, 1957).

References:

Minuchin, S. (1974). Families and family therapy. Cambridge, MA: Harvard University Press.
Jackson, D. D. (1957). The question of family homeostasis. Psychiatric Quarterly. Supplement, 31, 79–90.

Journal

28. **Who else is in your nuclear family (siblings, grandparents, etc.)? How do you feel about the family's *way of being* that has been created)?**

Are you the only one who is discontented with the family structure? If so, how do you feel about this? If not, who else? How do you feel about this?

In 1981, trough her research with children of alcoholics, Sharon Wegscheider-Cruse coined six terms for family roles. I will use her family roles to further explain dysfunctional family systems. Again, the roles come from the family's need for ***stability***, albeit through unhealthy relationships.

1. The **Dependent** (the person living with an addiction or addictive behavior)
2. The **Chief Enabler** (the person in denial or enabling the behavior of the dependent)
3. The **Hero** (The child that appears competent, serious, and overachieving, but may actually feel inadequate. This child is usually *parentified* (which will be explored in the next chapter).
4. The **Scapegoat** (the child that usually presents with defiant behaviors and attitudes. The family focuses the blame for problems on this child, rather than the alcoholic, or true problem.
5. The **Lost Child** (the child that is withdrawn and tends to do solitary activities, away from the family. They may not develop enough social skills, and may overcompensate by having a very active fantasy life.
6. The **Mascot** (the child that provides humor and distraction for the family. Although others are unable to take them seriously, they bring relief to the family (Wegscheider-Cruse, 1981).

References:
Wegscheider-Cruse, S. (1981), *Another Chance: Hope and Health for the Alcoholic Family*, Palo Alto, CA: Science and Behavior Books.

Journal

29. **Can you relate to any of the family roles? Which one and why? What are you thoughts and feelings about this?**

Journal

Being Parentified

It not your job to be your family's therapist. Many children become *parentified* or become the "hero" in their family, sacrificing their needs, and care-free childhood. *Parentification* was first coined in 1965 by Hungarian-American psychiatrist, Ivan Boszormeny-Nagu. He originally used the term to describe cases where parents use their children as substitutes for their own missing parents. These parents expect their children to fulfill the needs that their own parents did not meet.

In 1973, along with his colleague, Geraldine M. Spark, Boszormeny-Nagu elaborated on parentification as the unwanted and undeserved responsibility and pressure on a child to take care of their parents, siblings, or general household. As the parentified child, it becomes their job to help sustain the functioning of the family (and keep the *stability)*. It usually becomes an emotional weight that leads to feelings of resentment, anger, and sadness.

Boszormeny-Nagu and Spark also described parentification occurring when children meet their caregiver's emotional or psychological needs (usually unconsciously), like the need for distraction, relatedness, support, understanding, etc., (all the while, the child's emotional or psychological needs go unmet). In general, the parentified child's' efforts go unrewarded and unrecognized (1973).
With this in mind, look back at question 19, and re-answer!

The researchers also went further to explain that parentification can lead to some positive and beneficial consequences for the child in adulthood, especially in a career as a helping professional, in romantic relationships, or as a parent (Boszormeny-Nagu and Spark, 1973). Still, the negative effects live on.

In my experience as a Therapist, I have noticed the heartbreaking pain that parentified children and adult children carry with them, especially from not having the experience of *trusting* their caregiver to be reliable and available, which is an experience many children naturally crave from their parents. The safety, innocence, and freedom that comes with that security are missed. Even more troubling, I have noticed some parentified adult children **defend** against this pain by **normalizing** and **accepting** this imbalanced relationship--their parent needing from them, and not the other way around. With that dynamic, they learn to not need anything from their parents or anyone.

For children in immigrant, or socio-economic struggles, parentification may have been (and may continue to be) a requirement for the family's survival in society! It is understandable, especially when some families deal with racism, classism, sexism, etc. However, just because an injustice can be understood, does not mean it is right--it does not make the unpleasant consequences go away.

Again, the need to feel that you can **trust** and **rely** on your parent/s to meet some of *your* needs is a need in and of itself. This unmet need, whether folks repress it or not, is a form of a lost childhood and lost relationship that (like most lost things) needs to be mourned.

References:
Boszormenyi-Nagy, I. (1965). A theory of relationships: Experience and transaction. In I. Boszormenyi-Nagy & J. L. Framo (Eds.),*Intensive family therapy: Theoretical and practical aspects* (pp. 38-86). New York:Harper & Row.

Boszormenyi-Nagy, I., & Spark, G. M. (1973). *Invisible loyalties: Reciprocity in intergenerational family therapy*. Harper & Row.

Trying hard to change your parents and family can be a way that you continue to be parentified, continuing to meet your parent's needs, continue to be the "hero," continue to be controlling, and continue to not accept reality! Hence, you may need to stop trying and go through the grief of letting go (letting go of the responsibility you never deserved in the first place).

Journal

30. **Do you feel you were parentified as a child? Why or why not? How do you feel about this?**

Journal

31. **How have you tried to change or help your relationship with your parents, or family? How do you feel about this? How would it feel to stop trying? Would they then put in more effort?**

Journal

32. **How has your family role affected your life, relationships with others, personality, etc. How do you feel about this?**

Journal

33.**What would happen if your parents how you truly feel about them, your childhood, and the family dynamics? How would you feel? Do you think it would change anything? Or would it be harmful to you and your mental health?**

Defenses & Control

As you can see, childhood is a very vulnerable period in one's life because it is entirely defined by being helpless and dependent. The fear that you will not be helped or be able to depend on your caregiver is traumatizing

It is overwhelming and powerless for a small and vulnerable child to have such fears. It is so intolerable to believe in such a dreadful existence (where the person you need for survival, does not care about you, your emotions, or your stress). It is frightening to think this may be the world one lives in. Thus, in order to survive in such an environment, the child must create defenses to cope with their neglectful realities, and also feel a sense of control (rather than out of control or helpless). For example, *internalization* and becoming *parentified* can be viewed as defense mechanisms.

Some other defenses include *repression, denial, dissociation, distraction, avoidance, rationalization, intellectualization, internalization, overcompensation*, and *under-compensation*, etc.

Feel free to research some of these defenses to learn more. Ultimately, since most defense mechanisms occur *unconsciously* (out of one's awareness), professional intervention, like therapy, can help in exploring your defenses.

Acceptance

Feeling and accepting the sadness that your parents could not be the parents you wanted or deserved and that you will never have those parents can be extremely heartbreaking. The loss needs to be mourned. Going through the pain is the only way to make peace. You have to go *through* the emotions to finish it. You have to feel it to its end. Release it. Let it out.

Finish the feeling.

Of course, some feelings are never finished with you, and you may also have to accept and get comfortable with that (through patience and self-compassion).

Sometimes letting go of the unpleasant emotions you have towards someone who has caused you so much sorrow can be scary because it means *welcoming* reality and the truth--it means letting go of any attempt to deny or change your past.

Looking back at "Processing & Making Meaning," (pg 19) take *time to feel* your feelings and grieve about your loss.

Grieving

We all have a period in our life called "childhood," but when people say "I didn't have a childhood" or "I had a lost childhood," it seems they are insinuating that they did not have an innocent, safe, playful, responsibility-free childhood. (They did not have a secure childhood attachment). Hence, what makes folks feel they had a "lost childhood," is having an insecurely attached childhood-- unsafe, unpredictable, and sometimes responsibility-ridden, childhood.

Technically, all childhoods are lost to time, but having an insecure or emotionally neglectful childhood seems to be a form of death--a missed opportunity. When this occurs, it is not simply time that ends childhood, but the *traumatic childhood itself* that shatters the experience. Without it being mourned, the shattered pieces can freeze time--you can get stuck in the past. You have to collect the pieces back together and come back to your *true self*.

You can't fully grieve your lost childhood until you accept that the opportunity to repair is gone forever. That window of time is over. The chance for your parent to be there for you as a child is gone. The carefree and safe childhood that you wish you had (and that all children want and deserve), can no longer be.

Grieving your childhood also means letting go of your fantasy childhood and fantasy parents, which you may have held onto for far too long.

There is no time-table for how long your mourning will last or if it will ever end. The process of grieving can be nonlinear and have many ups and downs. Be patient with yourself. Eventually the intensity and duration of how sad you feel will shorten.

Although your childhood is gone, the wounded, inner child never dies--it is internalized inside of you, and it needs you to acknowledge it! It needs you to reparent it. The time to become emotionally connected with yourself (and others) is now.

Journal

34. **Would you describe your childhood as a lost childhood? Why or why not?**

How does it feel to grieve your childhood?

Journal

Rituals

With awareness and intentionality, rituals can help you mourn your childhood. Rituals are sentimental practices that mean something to you.

Rituals are a way to create a sense of acceptance, peace, and wholeness. They can be a way to *make time* to reflect and process your emotions. They can also be transformative and healing.

Journal

35. **Make up your own rituals for your healing process. Why have you chosen these practices?**

Empathy

Maintaining awareness of the external factors that have affected your parents emotional capabilities can help you build more **empathy** for your parents (and also for yourself). The traumas they may have survived may have caused them to become psychologically fragile and emotionally incapable. For example, some traumas may cause parents to have a poor sense of reality, or live in irrational, delusional, depressive, anxious, or narcissistic states of mind.

Having empathy for your parents also helps *depersonalize* their emotional distance or neglect.
Your parent's own abilities to emotionally connect is *about them, not about you*. You did not (and do not) deserve to be emotionally neglected.

Your parents have gone through some stuff. They are human beings with lives (and childhoods) before you! It is extremely tragic the pain that some parents have endured that leads them to repeat the same injuries towards their children.

You may have inherited a long intergenerational history of pain, but you do not need to continue it. Be proud of yourself for having the resilience and strength to try to stop the cycle!

Take a pause here and feel the sadness and grief for your parents and their childhood!

Take a pause here and feel the sadness and grief for yourself and your childhood!

Journal

36. **What are some of your parent's/s' past traumas or socio-economic-historical-psychological circumstances that you believe factor into their emotional disconnection with you?**

How does it feel to empathize with your parents?

Journal

Taking Action: Setting Realistic Expectations & Boundaries

Depending on how you describe or experience your relationship, you may feel you need to go "no-contact" or ***estrange*** yourself (completely remove yourself from your parent's life). This is valid action if you feel the current adult relationship is **abusive**, **manipulative**, **traumatizing**, and causing you **mental distress**.

Setting **emotional boundaries** and **realistic expectations** can help you be around your parents. Through grieving what you wish you had, and accepting what you do have, you can let go of any unrealistic expectations, and lean towards empathy and **forgiveness**.

But *forgiving if not forgetting*. Your parent/s may still be difficult to accept. Time has changed, but they have not. Hence, it can be painful to let go of your past resentment, while still being triggered and upset by their current behaviors. Because of this, you may need to further distance yourself from an already distant relationship. You will need to create the emotional and physical boundaries that help maintain your mental health.

Regardless of what actions or boundaries you put in place, I encourage therapy as a space to help you decide.

Accepting Ambivalence & Feeling Guilty

You will always have an emotional tie to your parents because they raised you; they're a part of your lived experience. Hence, you can feel love, care, and empathy for your parents, but, as noted, you are not responsible for meeting their needs. Feeling guilty about not meeting their needs is normal, especially if you've been accustomed to doing so since childhood. However, meeting your **own** needs means allowing yourself to be a child, not a parent, to your parents.

If your parents guilt-trip you over not giving them what they want or need, this is a form of manipulation, causing even more tension and resentment. (Hence, the importance of setting realistic expectations and boundaries).

Reparenting and grieving your childhood means accepting ambivalence--accepting both the pleasant (love and care) and unpleasant feelings you have about your parents. Ambivalence is not easy--it is uncomfortable. But give yourself the patience and compassion to tolerate all your emotions, including uncomfortable ones.

Still, if the connection is doing more harm than good, and you can not even tolerate a superficial relationship with your parents, you may have to go "no contact" to liberate yourself and finally have peace in your life.

Journal

37. **What emotional or physical boundaries would you like to put in place? How do you feel about this? Are your parents going to guilt-trip you or misunderstand your boundaries? How do you feel about this?**

Journal

Love

In the powerful song, "Godspeed," Frank Ocean* sings about one of life's persistent truths--some loves never go away--it's a mystery. In "Godspeed" there is grace, empathy, forgiveness, and honesty--all forms of love.

Journal

38. **Can you do this for your parents? For yourself? Can you mourn your childhood? Can you let go of the anger? The resentment? The sorrow? Can you reparent yourself? Can you (as an adult now) wish your parents well and set them free of your demands--wish them *godspeed*? Can you love them? Can you love yourself**?**

*...and James Blake with his powerful cover
**Loving yourself sometimes means letting go of an abusive relationship with your parents

Journal

Making Peace & Meaning

To truly wish someone well, you have to let go of the pain they've caused you. You may never get an apology from your parents concerning their parenting mistakes, or an acknowledgment of their emotional detachment or distance. They may in fact be content with the level of the emotional connection they have with you as a child, and adult! They may never understand or change.

But you can understand yourself and change! You can stay on the path towards peace of mind and peace of heart. So far in this guide, you have learned to find your peace through increasing your emotional connection with yourself, understanding your childhood, grieving your childhood, increasing acceptance, and learning to reparent yourself.

Making peace from an experience also means **making meaning.** Sometimes this meaning may simply be more self-understanding, hope, security, or it may increase your desire to be a better parent for your own children, better partner, or better human being. Making meaning from your emotions and experiences makes clear your beliefs, values, and future desires.

Journal

39. **What meaning (or change) do you make from everything that you have explored in this guide? How do you feel about this?**

Write a letter to your parent/s about all that you have discovered. Tell them how much the emotional distance has hurt, and your childhood experience. Express both your pleasant and unpleasant feelings. *Do not give your parent/s this letter.* The purpose of the letter is to help you internalize your growth and understand your new narrative. Your parent/s may not be ready for such a letter (or be emotionally capable). If you do ever want to give them this letter, I encourage you to attend therapy first.

Peace is a tranquil state without pain or anxiety. I can not guarantee your pain or anxiety about your parents will ever cease (much like grief). It's not easy. Therapy may be needed to help you continue your healing.

Still, I hope I have helped you get closer to equanimity.

Regardless if you ever make it to the destination, **relief** follows you along any path towards peace, which is better than any alternative.

So stay on the path!

Godspeed!

Journal

40. **Do you feel you have come closer to making peace with your relationship with your parent? How do you feel about this? Where on the path is the most difficult? What part of the path is most treacherous or painful? How will you continue to work on your journey towards peace?**

Journal

Your feedback matters to me! If you have a minute, please feel free to leave a review on Amazon, Bookshop, Goodreads, or wherever purchased!

Thank you!
Godspeed!

CPSIA information can be obtained
at www.ICGtesting.com
Printed in the USA
LVHW090147220821
695821LV00002B/214

9 781087 942926